BRITISH RAIL SCRAPBOOK 1955

John Adams & Patrick Whitehouse

LONDON

IAN ALLAN LTD

The ex-North British Railway 'Glen' class 4-4-0 was built for the West Highland Railway and representatives were seen at work on its tracks until the late 1950s. The coming of nationalisation saw the advent of the LMS Stanier Class 5 4-6-0s to the line and the consequent elimination of the old partnership of a 'Glen' and a Gresley K2 2-6-0. Sometimes however, an LNER pair was used and in August 1955 No 62482 *'Glen Mamie'* acted as pilot (the inside engine in old LNER practice) to K1 class 2-6-0 No 62012. This picture shows the 'Glen' backing on to the train at Fort William station.
Photo: P. B. Whitehouse.

First published 1976

ISBN 0 7110 0694 6

Published by Ian Allan Ltd, Shepperton, Surrey, and printed in the United Kingdom by Ian Allan Printing Ltd.

THE RAILWAY ENTHUSIAST'S YEAR 1955

The £1,240million British Railways Modernisation Plan was laid out by the British Transport Commission's Chairman, Sir Brian Robertson, on January 25. Numbed by successive governments' refusals to allow the railways any priority for capital investment and raw material, we gaped at the size of the purse. Innocently, we assumed that behind the re-equipment proposals the BTC had a fully-worked out strategy which really would, in the plan's words, 'recover the ground that has been lost to other forms of transport over the past 30 years.'

The BTC, alas, had no such strategy, though this did not dawn on us until the 1960s. Hardware was made an end in itself, not the means to an end. Railwaymen could conceive of only one way to run a railway — the way they always had: all that had to be done was to just change steam for diesel or electric engines, semaphore for colour-light signals, build new stations and depots, and the millenium would follow as surely as the night the day.

A number of the plan's items were, in fact, just pre-war projects dusted off with little or no re-editing. Since the BTC admitted that the plan would take at least 15 years to complete, they were sanguinely expecting that the competitive transport situation would be roughly the same in 1970 as it was in 1939. Everything would just be going a bit faster. And the Government believed them: Parliament was assured by the Minister that there was every hope of the loaned capital being repaid with interest by 1970.

Much of the plan's re-equipment is now *fait accompli* — but not all. There is still no electrification from Kings Cross to Doncaster, Leeds and possibly York; GE suburban electrification has yet to reach Ipswich, Harwich and Felixstowe; and the Oxted line remains a diesel enclave in the Southern's third-rail network, though the Waterloo-Weymouth line *is* electric as far as Bournemouth, whereas the plan marked it off for dieselisation. Above all, we still await elimination of what Sir Brian Robertson damned at the plan's launching as the 'appalling handicap of Emmett-like trains going clanketty-clank through our countryside, which make it impossible for BR to give a first-class freight service' — the unfitted, loose-coupled freight train.

New steam power was still coming off the production lines as 1955 opened. Crewe works was rolling out Class 9 2-10-0s for the Eastern, London Midland and North Eastern Regions and was soon to start on the 10 Crosti-boilered 2-10-0s, Nos 92020-9, for the Midland line of the LMR. Darlington was assembling BR standard Class 2 2-6-0s for the North Eastern and Scottish Regions; Derby, Doncaster and Brighton BR standard Class 4 2-6-4Ts for the Eastern, North Eastern, Scottish and Southern Regions; and Swindon BR standard Class 3 2-6-2Ts and 16XX class 0-6-0PTs for the Western Region. Derby and Doncaster were to turn next to batches of new Class 5 4-6-0s for the London Midland, Scottish and Southern Regions, and Doncaster had a subsequent order of Class 4 2-6-0s for the Southern and North Eastern Regions. Swindon was due to build further Class 4 4-6-0s for the Southern, some Class 9 2-10-0s for the Eastern and a last batch of 94XX 0-6-0Ts for the Western Region. Crewe was set for its last taper-boiler 'Royal Scot' conversion, of No 46137, and the solitary BR standard Class 8 Pacific, No 71000 *Duke of Gloucester*, was being probed by the Swindon engineers in a series of stationary and track tests that would conclude with haulage of 20 coach loads.

Derby's first diesel multiple-units had been shown off in the spring of 1954, then inaugurated dmu service in the West Riding. The second batch took over the Carlisle-Silloth service in November, then spread on to the Penrith-Workington and Carlisle lines in January, ousting in the process two of BR's most photographed steam veterans, Nos 58409/12, two of the last ex LNWR 'Cauliflower' 0-6-0s (one more survived at Widnes). In the course of 1955 the dmus were to transform the railway scene successively in Lincolnshire, East Anglia, Lancashire and on Tees-side.

Some fallible memories nowadays believe the axe was not flung about to any purpose until Beeching took control. Not so. In the first five years of nationalisation the BTC approved closure of nearly 100 passenger services. By the end of 1954 it had shut down 324 passenger stations and just short of 1,500 route-miles to passenger traffic (though, granted, the network still totalled 19,150 route-miles at that date), and the new year had opened with a fresh clutch of closure announcements. Many of the closures were fiercely contested — and delayed — at Transport Users' Consultative Committee hearings, for by early 1955 the BR publicity machine was feeding the protesters with handy ammunition in its proud but misleading statistics of the hordes of new traffic generated by the first diesel multiple-units. These, we persuaded ourselves, would be the salvation of the stopping train. There was fierce pressure, too, for railbus-and-unmanned-halt operation of rural branches on the German pattern.

January was darkened by a disaster at Sutton Coldfield which killed 17, including three enginemen. The 12.15pm York-Bristol, headed by Class 5 4-6-0 No 45274, had been diverted via Lichfield and Aston because of engineering work at Tamworth. Inexplicably, the conductor driver — who was actually driving, because the rostered driver had broken the rules and retired to the train — entered the sharp 30mph-restricted curve into the station at nearer 60mph and the engine and first few coaches were strewn about the platform ends. The men on the footplate were killed.

Incidental January observation included the first rostered working of a Stanier Pacific into Manchester since the war, coming in on the Friday 6.45am from Crewe so as to take on the 5.50pm Manchester-Euston and the Saturday 11.45am back, after which the engine withdrew to Crewe on the Saturday 5.45pm from Manchester. On the ER, the infamous 'sit up-and-beg' Kings Cross suburban articulated train-sets, with their penitentially cramped compartments, were at last being supplanted by five-coach sets of new standard BR non-corridor stock; two Fowler 2-6-4Ts, Nos 42328/74, were short-stay allocations to Hitchin shed at this time.

In 1955 BR had just seven main-line diesel locomotives. Smallest was No 10800, an 827hp diesel-electric branch-line prototype originated by the LMS, but not delivered until 1950; after a spell on Tilbury line passenger haulage early in the year, it migrated to Rugby in February to take over a Class 5 4-6-0 diagram extending to Peterborough and Birmingham. Second of the diesel units at this time was the unique Fell diesel-mechanical 2-B-B-2, No 10100, another LMS idea that took shape in 1951; in the spring of 1955 it was working between Derby and Manchester, apart from dynamometer car tests betweeen Skipton and Carlisle at the end of April. Finally there were the two LMS Co-Co prototypes, Nos 10000/1, the Southern 1,750hp 1Co-Co1 twins of 1951, Nos 10201/2, and the later Southern 2,000hp 1Co-Co1 No 10203 of 1954 — all five diesel-electrics. Since the spring of 1953 this last quintet had been based on the Southern Region's Nine Elms depot to operate Waterloo-Exeter and Waterloo-Bournemouth

rosters, but in March Nos 10000/1 and 10201/2 returned to West Coast main line operation from Camden, and were followed across the Thames in July by No 10203. Later in the year, in September, No 10203 was to be tried on a daily Euston-Glasgow out-and-home roster of over 800 miles in 24hr, down on the 12.20am sleeper from London and back on the 'Mid-day Scot'.

Spring announcements of impending closures included one of subsequent import for the 1970s. The Southern Region proclaimed withdrawal from June 13 of all trains between East Grinstead and Lewes, setting the stage for emergence of today's Bluebell Railway — but not until a lengthy tragi-comedy of objections to the proposal had been played out.

A sporting fixture that all North London enthusiasts underscored in their diaries was the women's hockey international at Wembley. It attracted trainloads of fans from most points of the compass and a delightfully cosmopolitan assembly of power on Neasden shed. On March 12, 1955, Neasden's guests included: from the Western, 'County' No 1025 and two 'Halls', Nos 6921 and 6938; from the Southern, four 'Schools' 4-4-0s, Nos 30904 of St Leonards and 30912/7/8 of Ramsgate; and from distant parts of the Eastern, A3 Pacific No 60046 of Doncaster and B17 4-6-0s Nos 61614/8 off the GE line. At this time the London end of the GC line was once more getting a frequent sight of North Eastern Class B16 4-6-0s, filling in time on Marylebone passenger trains or London freights after bringing a North-East-to-South-West freight to the inter-Regional transfer yard at Woodford Halse.

Weatherwise it had been a pretty daunting first quarter. In Scotland, fierce blizzards had first swept Caithness and Sutherland in mid-January, piling up drifts as deep as 25ft on the Helmsdale-Wick and Thurso line. Despite frenzied shuttling to and fro of snowploughs, three Highland trains were stuck fast at different points for nearly 24hr. In mid-February Arctic conditions again enveloped the Far North, this time more severe than anyone could remember. By dawn on February 17 three overnight Highland freight trains and two snowploughs were embedded. Later that day the 3.10pm Inverness-Tain had to give up at Alness and its 42 passengers camped out the night in the station. This was Friday. Not until the afternoon of the following Sunday did ploughs and gangs of men, burrowing into drifts up to 500yds long and 12ft high, manage to clear the whole line from Perth to Wick and Thurso.

Four days later the Darlington-Penrith line over the Pennines was submerged in snow and a freight, a plough, their engines and two more engines on banking duty were stranded. Kirkby shed decided on strong-arm tactics. For maximum impact on the drifts it packed three Class 2 2-6-0s between its two large

The Sutton Coldfield disaster, January 1955. Lifting some of the wreckage.
Photo: J. Ellson.

ploughs, and an awe-inspiring show they put up. Shrieking their hooters continuously at each other in a code to signify 'forward', 'back' or 'ease couplings', the trio would charge the drifts in a fury of barking exhausts and cinders, pound away until they stalled, then withdraw to mount a fresh attack. Double-track was not restored over the smmmit until the second week of March. Soon afterward yet more heavy snow blocked the West Coast main line between Ecclefechan and Lockerbie, with the result that the Waverley route unusually witnessed a couple of 'Duchess' Pacifics, Nos 46221/30, and 'Princess' Pacific No 46203 as well as several 'Royal Scots' hauling diverted traffic on March 21.

Sound and smoke erupted in Birmingham's outskirts on two March Sundays as Class 5 No 44776 and 'Jubilee' No 45554 were set at the Lickey Incline for unaided climbs and re-starts on the bank with, respectively, seven- and eight-coach loads of 222/252 tons including dynamometer car. The Class 5 overcame some initial slipping to achieve its re-starts on the incline successfully, but the 'Jubilee' had much more trouble, at one stage having to back its train down to Bromsgrove for a fresh attack.

A major spring event was the loan to the Western for a month's trials of Stanier 'Duchess' Pacific No 46237, which arrived at Old Oak shed on April 19. The WR's 'Kings' were steaming indifferently on postwar coal and Swindon thought the 'Duchess' layout worth study as a latter-day extension by Stanier of Churchward principles. Manned by a Western crew, the visitor sampled all three main routes from Paddington—to Birmingham, Bristol and Plymouth — and amongst its assignments wore the 'Cornish Riviera' headboard.

The stranger took the customary help over the South Devon inclines, so that lineside watchers between Newton Abbot and Plymouth saw it incongruously coupled inside 'Castle' 4-6-0 No 5019 on the down 'Riviera' of May 17, for instance, and paired with 'Hall' 4-6-0 No 5915 on the up train next day. No 46237's performance was disappointingly variable and its thirst tended to outrun the WR spacing of water troughs, forcing an out-of-course stop for water on one run; but it put up at least one memorable performance on the 'Cornish Riviera', lifting 420tons over Whiteball summit at a minimum of 46mph. Swindon drew one lesson from Stanier, for later in the year came the first double-chimney modification of a 'King', No 6015, with outstanding results.

Conversely, it looked as though some WR 4-6-0s might be playing to a new audience when 'Grange' 4-6-0 No 6865 was put through clearance tests at Clapham Junction on April 18. But there must have been snags; through working via the West London line on to the SR's Central Section with inter-Regional

traffic by these engines never materialised.

Two more pre-grouping inside-cylinder 4-4-0 classes were dismissed from active service with withdrawal of SR Class L12 No 30434 in February and Class E 4-4-0 No 31166 in May, but there were still enough examples of this vintage arrangement about to diversify the lineside show. On Fridays, for instance, West Riding enthusiasts would look for the 8.55am Newcastle-Liverpool, because a Selby 4-4-0 had to be got home from an early morning workmen's train and that usually led to the oddlooking match between Ripon and Leeds of an ex-North Eastern Railway Class D20 4-4-0 with a Heaton Class V2 2-6-2 or Pacific, which might be a Class A2/3, A3 or A4. From early March Didcot had the interest of daily visits from an ex-LSWR Class T9 4-4-0 of Eastleigh returning to Didcot, Newbury & Southampton line passenger turns after two years' absence, but this time handled by WR enginemen between Didcot and Newbury.

On the LMR, compound 4-4-0s could be still spotted as express passenger pilots on both West Coast and Midland main lines; until the autumn of 1955, in fact, compounds at Bedford were still the unaided rostered power for the town's two peak expresses to St Pancras, the 8.6 and 8.25am. In the North, a Class 2 4-4-0 and 'Royal Scot' 4-6-0 pairing became a daily autumn spectacle between Carlisle and Leeds, as the train's 11coach formation consistently exceeded a 'Scot's' 350ton limit over the Pennine climbs; the 4-4-0, from Carlisle Kingmoor shed, returned home by stages on stopping trains, with an overnight stay at Hellifield.

Trains Illustrated gave the West Midlands a spectacle to remember on April 16 when it ran its 'Lickey Limited' special on a triangular Paddington-Bristol-Birmingham-Paddington itinerary with 'Castle' 4-6-0 power throughout, except over parts of the Birmingham network — notably the New Street tunnels — where tight clearances defeated the stranger. The train was tailed by one of the ex-LNER 'Coronation' beaver-tail observation cars, whose occupants were exhilarated by an unforgettable close-up of 'Big Bertha', the Midland's 0-10-0 Lickey banker, in full cry as the cavalcade clambered up the 1 in 37¾ bank from Bromsgrove. With 'Castle' No 7017 in strident lead, the Lickey Hills were certainly alive with the sound of music — and to fair purpose, for the 330ton train was taken over the top at a minimum of 24½mph. At Bournville the 'Castle' was replaced by a Class 5 for a circuit via Grand Junction and the Camp Hill avoiding line on to the ex-GW main line on the London side of Bordesley, where No 7017 resumed charge for the return to Paddington.

Within a month or so Bromsgrove was aghast at rumours that 'Big Bertha' was to be scrapped. Local

Above: 'Castle' class 4-6-0 No 7017 *G. J. Churchward* nearing Blackwell with the Ian Allan 'Lickey Limited' on 16 April 1955 with 0-10-0 Lickey Banker at rear.
Photo: W. A. Camwell.

Below: Bournville, 16 April 1955 with 'Castle' class No 7017 *G. J. Churchward* about to come off the 'Lickey Limited'. Clearance problems did not allow the locomotive to work into Birmingham, New Street.
Photo: T. J. Edgington.

drivers set about petitioning the authorities for a reprieve and, hedging their bets, planned a mammoth wake for the engine, but the 0-10-0 had only been stopped for a boiler examination. The alarm had been sounded by the return to Bromsgrove in August of the ex-LNER 2-8-8-2 Garratt, No 69999, now converted for oil-burning, and the arrival of a BR Class 9 2-10-0, No 92008, as deputy for the 0-10-0 while the latter was stopped. But both usurpers retired within a few weeks. The Garratt proved a refractory steamer on oil and retreated back to Gorton, to be scrapped at the year's end, while the 2-10-0 was said to lack the 0-10-0's punch as a freight train banker. Talking of Garratts, the LMR announced its first withdrawals from their class of these engines, Nos 49785/90, in July.

In May Midland enthusiasts goggled at a new 2-10-0 variant that disgorged its exhaust, not from a front-end chimney like a Christian design, but out of an ugly coal scuttle-shaped device near the rear of a mis-shapen boiler. The first of the 10 Crosti-boilered engines had been delivered to Wellingborough. In an effort to conserve energy, the Crosti boiler re-used the firebox gases. Instead of ejecting them straight from the tubes to the atmosphere, the Crosti arrangement re-directed them through a secondary drum beneath the main boiler to pre-heat the feed water, then into a final smokebox immediately ahead of the firebox, from which they were expelled to atmosphere through an ungainly chimney slotted into the running plate. The 2-10-0s' crews were soon complaining bitterly that the exhaust was billowing straight into the cab and before long the engines were stopped for the addition of deflector plates to the rear chimneys.

Sheer recklessness caused the year's second serious derailment through excessive speed, at Wormit, Fife, on May 28. A tender-first Class 5 4-6-0, No 45458, took the sharply curved approach to the Tay Bridge at 40-45 instead of the prescribed 10mph and spread itself and the first four coaches of a packed return excursion from Tayport over the platforms. Evidence showed the driver had an irresponsible record; he had been drinking between out and home legs of the run and moreover was entertaining an unauthorised adult and child passenger on the footplate; both gatecrashers were killed with the fireman.

An inflow of BR standard types was steadily changing the face of several Southern traffic areas. The Oxted line was getting to know the Class 4 2-6-4Ts and the South Devon branches were resounding to the chirrup of Class 3 2-6-2Ts instead of the throaty exhaust of Class M7 0-4-4Ts (though in the summer of 1955 Exeter's solitary Class O2 0-4-4T still made a day's work of the Exmouth branch pick-up freight). Class 4 2-6-0s were ousting SR Moguls from Reading-Redhill line duties and now the 'King Arthurs'' days

were clearly numbered with the arrival at Stewarts Lane and later Nine Elms of the Region's first standard Class 5 4-6-0s (even so, the Eastern Section still had to turn out Class E1 and D1 4-4-0s, as well as all manner of SR 2-6-0s and 'Schools' 4-4-0s, to cope with the 1955 summer peak Continental and Kent Coast traffic).

At the same time a revision of the Oxted line services had congregated an attractive bunch of old-timers at Tunbridge Wells shed to deal with a new pattern of connecting links between there and Oxted. As well as Class H and M7 0-4-4Ts the gathering included the last ex-LCD Class R 0-4-4T, No 31666, and the sole surviving ex-LBSC Class D3 0-4-4T, No 32390; this last pair of veterans was withdrawn in the autumn. And despite the new 2-6-4Ts, one could still find ex-LBSC Class E4 0-6-2Ts coping with additional Saturday passenger trains on the Tunbridge Wells-Eastbourne line and its gradients as steep as 1 in 50, even covering the Birkenhead-Brighton through train from Redhill onwards in the height of the summer.

Long-running rumour that the Board's traction chiefs intended to rebuild the Bulleid Pacifics of the Southern was confirmed during the summer. The reasoning was clear when the BTC released another of its comprehensively detailed bulletins on locomotives subjected to performance and efficiency tests, first on the stationary plant at Swindon or Rugby, then on the steeply-graded Skipton-Carlisle route. No 10 in the BTC series dealt with the 'Merchant Navy' class, of which No 35022 had been sampled on the rollers at Rugby and then on the open road. In brief, Bulleid's design was applauded for a boiler with almost unlimited steaming capacity, though at heavy cost in coal consumption, and damned for its chain-driven valve-gear, which was so erratic in working that successive days' testing in near-identical conditions produced quite contradictory results. Other Bulleid departures from orthodox practice came in for criticism. For instance, the Pacific's full potential was never measured, because oil from the bath enclosing the chain-driven gear would escape on to the driving-wheel treads and, if the regulator was opened wide, set up a slipping so savage that it buckled the side-rods more than once; this was a not infrequent occurrence in normal Southern Region service, either.

Just as the BTC was increasing all passenger and freight charges (third-class travel was up from 1·75 to 1·88 old pence — or 0·94p — a mile and first-class from 2·62 to 2·82d, or 1·18p) and the summer timetables were imminent, footplatemen hit the country with its first official countrywide rail stoppage since 1926. The previous winter the NUR had rejected new terms, threatened a strike, then won an improved offer from a Court of Enquiry. Such special treatment for

Above: Ex-LNER Garratt No 69999 banking a Bristol-Birmingham express on Lickey incline (note that the Garratt is doing all the work).
Photo: P. B. Whitehouse.

Below: The first rumours of alarm that the old Lickey 'banker' No 58100 was to be retired and scrapped became serious in 1955 when, in fact, the old lady went to Derby works for her last repair. She is seen there, minus her headlamp — an ominous sign.
Photo: J. Ellson

NUR grades aggrieved ASLEF, who complained that the traditional skill differentials between enginemen and the rest had been intolerably narrowed thereby. Rebuffed by the BTC, ASLEF called a strike for May 1, but was then persuaded to call it off for fresh talks. A last-ditch BTC compromise that in effect conceded extra pay for higher-grade enginemen only was rejected and ASLEF ordered all its members out on Whit-Saturday.

The stoppage lasted 17 days. As in recent times, London commuter services were the worst sufferers; the Liverpool Street suburban service, for instance, was virtually immobile, with a solitary motorman at work on the Shenfield line, and the SR could only muster about 10 motormen at depots covering the Waterloo suburban services. But though many sheds obeyed the strike call 100 per cent, others were in two minds and a considerable number of enginemen who were NUR members stayed on the job. Moreover, as the strike dragged on BR operators grew more adept at pulling together the threads of available resources. On Whit-Monday only some 1,200 passenger and 200 freight trains were run, but by June 4 BR was managing to move in a day over 4,200 passenger and nearly 3,000 freight trains even though only 11,100 enginemen and cleaners were active out of nearly 80,000 on the books; and by June 11 the number of passenger trains had been lifted to 7,800.

Needless to say, the 17 days' operational improvisation generated plenty of entertainment for lineside watchers. On the first Saturday of the strike, for instance, the cancellation of a West Midlands extra found its rostered 'King' coupled to another on the 2.10pm Paddington-Birkenhead so as to get both of them, Nos 6001/14, back to Stafford Road shed, Wolverhampton for the duration. For the first time, Liverpool Street-Southend Victoria services were graced by 'Britannia' Pacifics. In the West Riding most of the new diesel multiple-units were inactive, so a Class N1 0-6-2T, No 69474, came huskily back to work on a Whit-Monday Leeds-Bradford shuttle service. (Incidentally, the West Riding's favourite N1 workings, on the Bradford-Halifax-Keighley trains, had just been laid to rest with the services' withdrawal on May 21. Within a few weeks the BR publicity machine was proudly trumpeting statistics of hugely increased takings on the Leeds-Bradford service following the dmu takeover, which aroused heated protest that the Bradford-Halifax-Keighley trains had been blindly axed.)

The strike left ugly scars in lost traffic. Grimsby, in particular, was never the same again as a railway centre. Many fish merchants had switched to road and did not return to rail, setting off a downward spiral in the economics of the port's famous fish trains which eventually drove them from the timetables. It helped BR lose 10 per cent of the merchandise and livestock traffic the railways had carried in 1954.

The summer timetables, (introduction of which had to be deferred for some days because of the dispute) killed one Pullman train and gave birth to another. The casualty was the 'Devon Belle', a service which flattered to deceive with initially substantial loadings on its 1947 debut, then gradually lost out to the private car. The Plymouth portion was shed in 1950 but as an exclusively Waterloo-Ilfracombe train the 'Belle' still lost money; it barely evaded abolition in 1952, but lingered on as a weekend service only. It was historic for its avoidance of a public stop at Salisbury, the midway Waterloo-Exeter engine change being made at Wilton; and for its two Pullman observation cars, which after the 'Belle's' demise were refurbished in BR livery and despatched to the scenic West Highland and Kyle of Lochalsh routes in Scotland. Newcomer was the 'South Wales Pullman' between Paddington and Swansea, the first Pullman venture on GWR metals since the short-lived 'Torquay Pullman' of 1929. Its eight-car set was 'Castle' 4-6-0 – hauled and included *Diamond*, formerly the 'New Century Bar' on the SR's Dover-Ostend boat trains but with its bar section now redecorated and appropriately retitled 'Daffodil Bar'.

In the new schedules the East Coast Route pioneered an idea subsequently embraced by every major Western European railway — the car-sleeper. Brainchild of the Eastern Region's passenger management, the first train operated twice weekly between Kings Cross and Perth, loading its cars at the London end in the bay on the western side of the suburban station. In those days single-deck bogie vans with end doors were used for car-carrying and the inclusive return fare for car and driver was a modest £15, for passengers £4.50 each.

Another nostalgic memory is the London-Glasgow or Edinburgh return fare charged on the 'Starlight Specials'. These were bargain overnight weekend trains by the slower Anglo-Scottish routes — the Midland and GSW, and the GC from Marylebone into' the North Eastern Region — which had been introduced the previous summer. The trains were all third-class ordinary day coaches (re-designation of third as second class did not come until June, 1956), but supported by a buffet car. The 'Starlights' were back in the 1955 summer timetable, despite suspicions that they were being operated below cost — not surprisingly when the return fare was pitched as low as £3.50.

Over the previous year or so schedules had been perking up, but it was still news when a start-to-stop timing just crept over the mile-a-minute mark. The entire new timetable showed only 51 runs at 60mph or more, aggregating 5,510 miles, compared with 116

Above: Class M7 0-4-4T No 30242 on the 10.45 am Portsmouth all stations to Eastleigh train. Photo: P. M. Alexander

Below: Rebuilt Bullied Pacific No 35018 *British India Line* leaving Bournemouth Central, with the up 'Bournemouth Belle'. Photo: C. F. H. Oldham.

totalling 12,016 back in 1939. The best over the 44.1mile Darlington-York speedway in 1955, for instance, was 41min (by the down 'Tees-Tyne Pullman') and even on this stretch the timebooks showed only 14 daily runs at 60mph average or better.

Postwar operating and timekeeping were still lax enough to temper any clamour for tighter schedules. At the start of the year, for instance, the *Birmingham Post* had monitored the arrivals in Birmingham of the two-hour trains to and from London by both routes. During the four weeks of January the *average* lateness of the five down trains from Euston had ranged from 8¾ to 21min, of the five up trains to Euston from 6½ to 16½min; on the Western the three down trains were all 17½-18½min late on average, the two up trains to Paddington 18¼-20¾min late on average. A *Railway Magazine* reader groaned that on 10 trips within two months by an evening Doncaster-Kings Cross express he had been twice 15min late, twice 30min, four times 45min and twice 50min late. 'If this is the best that can be achieved by an A4 Pacific on a schedule which allows 200min for the 156miles with three intermediate stops totalling 16min and a not immoderately heavy load,' he grunted, 'things are in a bad way.' By the early summer, however, the late Cecil J. Allen was able to report that one of the worst operating offenders, the Western Division of the LMR, had effected a 'revolutionary' improvement in timekeeping.

The 'Elizabethan's' 6½hr booking for the 392.9miles from Kings Cross to Edinburgh non-stop in 1955 was unchanged from the previous summer, and an acceleration of the 'Flying Scotsman' could not better 4hr 40min down and 4hr 36min up for the 268.3 non-stop miles between Kings Cross and Newcastle. However a cut of the 'Scotsman's' overall schedule to 7hr ended a situation that had acutely embarrassed East Coast enthusiasts since the start of the previous timetable, when the LMR decided to perpetuate the up 'Royal Scot's' summer Glasgow-Euston schedule of 7¼hr, thereby getting its 10am departure from Glasgow into London 21min ahead of the 10am from Edinburgh. The up 'Mid-day Scot', too, was given an edge over the mid-day 'Heart of Midlothian' of the East Coast partners. No one living in apple-green territory could remember when they were last shamed this way. Fastest timings on the East Coast in the 1955 summer were by the morning and evening 'Bradford Flyers', booked to average 66.4mph down and 65.5mph up over the 106.7 miles between Hitchin and Retford.

Elsewhere on the LMR, the fastest Liverpool-Euston time was 3hr 25min, by the 5.25pm up 'Red Rose', and from Manchester to Euston 3½hr, by the 7.55am; one must remember, though, that some trainloads were massive — in particular, Pacifics were

regularly faced with 16-coach, 500ton loads on the businessmen's 7.55am Euston-Manchester and Liverpool, to be hauled over the 140.7 miles from Watford Junction to Crewe in 136min. The Western took the national laurels with the down 'Bristolian', booked from Paddington to Bristol via Bath at 67.6mph and back via Badminton at 67.2mph. The 'Cornish Riviera' was at last back on a four-hour Paddington-Plymouth timing, booked over the 193.6miles to Newton Abbot in 3hr 12min; the 'Pembroke Coast Express' was quickened to an unprecedented booking of 2hr 8min for the 133.4miles from Paddington to Newport; and for the first time since 1939 Oxford was blessed with a 60min train to Paddington, the 4pm from Worcester. The Southern's one and only mile-a-minute booking was the 'Atlantic Coast Express' allowance of 83min for the 83.7 miles from Waterloo to Salisbury.

Another nasty derailment was reported on August 7, about three miles south of Rugby on the GC line. The 10.35am Manchester-Marylebone was running over an hour late on the wrong line south of Rugby because engineering works were enforcing single-line operation. Instead of proceeding with caution, as the rules dictated in such circumstances, the experienced Neasden driver of Class V2 2-6-2 No 60828 inexplicably forged up to 50mph-plus. At that pace he ripped into the facing crossing at Barby Sidings that was returning him to the right line. The engine and several coaches plunged down an embankment, but the only fatality was the driver, who probably missed a notice shortening the single-line section and was not expecting to be switched at Barby Sidings. The official enquiry unearthed a good deal of laxity by other railway personnel that contributed to the disaster.

Few centres rivalled Aberdeen as a meeting-place of the traction majors. The local Ferryhill shed's only Pacifics were a few Class A2s, but Haymarket would send its A3 and occasionally its A4 Pacifics down the East Coast route to the Granite City; usually Tyneside-based Pacifics penetrated no further north than Dundee, but occasionally Thompson and Peppercorn Pacifics from Newcastle would add further spice to the ex-LNER scene at Aberdeen — on July 30, for instance, A1 No 60154 of Gateshead awas at the head of the southbound 'Aberdonian'. The ex-LMS route from Perth and Glasgow could itself sometimes turn up a Gresley Pacific, as when Haymarket A3 No 60101 brought the down 'Granite City' into Aberdeen from Glasgow Buchanan Street on September 5. Its contribution was more usually Stanier 'Duchesses' — sometimes from as far afield as Camden, for the London's shed's Pacifics headed the 'Royal Scot' right through to Glasgow in summer — that were appropriated to cover the 7.15am from Buchanan Street

Above: In 1955 the Western Region took the national laurels for speed with this train; the down 'Bristolian' was booked from Paddington to Bristol via Bath at an average speed of 67.6 mph. The engine is No 7025 *Sudeley Castle*.
Photo: P. M. Alexander.

Below: The down 'Royal Scot' climbing Shap behind 'Duchess' Pacific No 46227 *Duchess of Devonshire*.
Photo: Eric Treacy.

and the 3.30pm 'West Coast Postal' back from Glasgow, or elsewhere filling in during the day between nocturnal Crewe-Perth through sleeper workings. One 'Duchess' visitor was incongruously mated on July 16, when No 46225 was seen piloting standard Class 5 No 73006 out of Aberdeen on the up 'Granite City'. 'Britannia' Pacifics from Polmadie were just beginning to make the odd acquaintance with Aberdeen and on July 16 the city had its first recorded visit from the solitary BR Class 8 Pacific, No 71000, which had been deputed to the Crewe-Perth diagram since mid-June.

The unique 4-6-4, No 60700, derailed on facing points and overturned with the first two coaches of its train, the 3.50pm Kings Cross-Leeds, soon after leaving Peterborough on September 1. Happily there were no serious injuries, as speed was barely 20mph. The cause was total fracture of the right-hand leading bogie frameplate. The bogie was of unique pattern and the failure unprecedented, but those of ex-LNER Classes D49 and B17 had a similar strengthening of mild steel stretchers, designed at Darlington, as did a number of older engines. Examinations of all locomotives with similar bogie arrangements were promptly ordered, but the only significant casualties to be black-marked out of service as a result were the SR's Brighton Atlantics, early in 1956.

A special organised by Alan Pegler from the provinces to the (then) annual SBAC Farnborough Air Show was becoming a September feature. In 1955, on September 11, Pegler secured two Class D11 'Director' 4-4-0s, Nos 62666/7, to double-head from Doncaster to Basingstoke and back a lush rake that included a sleeper, two kitchen cars, a buffet car, an 'Elizabethan' bar-lounge and ex-'Coronation' beaver-tail observation car. The route from Doncaster was via Tuxford, Mansfield and Kirkby South Junction on to the GC line and thence to Banbury and Reading. In the following month the original ten 'Director' 4-4-0s of Class D10 were extinguished by withdrawal of No 62653.

There was precious little to fire the blood in the 1955 winter timetables. Incredibly the 'Flying Scotsman' was decelerated a half-hour and more to a 7½hr London-Edinburgh schedule northbound and 7hr 35min southbound, so that it became 60-65min slower than the summer non-stop 'Elizabethan' with only intermediate stops at Grantham and Newcastle and an increase of its limited load from 12 to 13 cars (grossing 480tons, however) to account for the discrepancy. (It was an ironic coincidence — in hindsight — that the prototype English Electric 'Deltic' diesel took the rails a month later!) The LMR managed a modest St Pancras-Sheffield improvement, but the Yorkshire city's best journey times from London of 3¼hr from St. Pancras by the 12noon, and 3hr 10min

by through coaches, detached at Retford, off the 7.50 Kings Cross-Leeds and Bradford, were still inferior to Midland, GC and GN performance before the Grouping, let alone LMS and LNER timings before 1939. Elsewhere, the WR made reconstruction of Banbury station the excuse for killing off every one of the Paddington-Birmingham 2hr schedules.

The autumn was enlivened by recurrent tales of three-figure speed on the Western. Some originated from travellers on the 'Bristolian', which had reverted to consistent 'Castle' haulage, and by specially selected engines of that class from Old Oak in the down direction, and Bristol Bath Road, in the up. Supporting evidence was hard to come by and some accounts strained credulity to the limit — in particular, a persistent rumour that the first double-chimney 'King', No 6015, had been whipped up to 110mph with the 'Cornish Riviera' on the gentle, 4½mile down-grade to Curry Rivell Junction, on the Paddington-Exeter main line; an even more far-fetched claim of 116mph on a special test run was published. Some of these stories were probably traceable to the determination of Paddington, Swindon and their more fanatical friends to keep the old Great Western image burnished. Other manifestations that year were the upgrading of 'Halls' and 'County' 4-6-0s from mixed traffic black to passenger green livery — and, of course, the still relentless denigration of the BR standard Pacifics throughout the Region.

As the evenings lengthened, lineside observations that lingered in the mind included the arrival for shunting trial at Kentish Town and at Liverpool Bank Hall shed of SR 'USA' class 0-6-0Ts Nos 30061/6 respectively (diesel shunters were starting to supersede the type at Southampton Docks). On September 23 SR Class T9 4-4-0 No 30304 was specially dispatched to Shrewsbury to work the Talyllyn Railway Preservation Society's annual special thence to Towyn over the Cambrian; the train had been brought down from Paddington by 'Star' 4-6-0 No 4061. In mid-October 'Royal Scot' 4-6-0 No 46120 was based at Derby and made the type's debut over the Peak Forest main line to Manchester. Later in the month, on October 27, a 'Clan' Pacific, No 72007, raised eyebrows at Euston and in early November the southern end of the West Coast main line had another surprise when Toton's Garratts, edged out of their Midland main line coal haulage by new 2-10-0s, started trundling coal up to Willesden.

Ex-LNER Class B12/3 4-6-0s at Peterborough Spital Bridge shed had been working through to Rugby and Northampton on cross-country services since August, but a much more ex-GE unlikely visitor to the Midland line in mid-December was Class E4 2-4-0 No 62786, one of the Cambridge stud of the type for that area's rural branch workings; No 62786

Above: The prototype English Electric 'Deltic' diesel took to the rails during the winter of 1955 and is seen passing Rugby.
Photo: Colin P. Walker.

Below: Ex-LSWR T9 class 4-4-0 No 30304 on a chartered Talyllyn Railway Preservation Society special train passing Aberdovey golf links on 23 September. The train ran from London to Shrewsbury behind GWR 'Star' class 4-6-0 No 4061 *Glastonbury Abbey*.
Photo: P. B. Whitehouse.

had been hurriedly substituted for a failure on a Cambridge-Kettering train and was then appropriated by the Midland to head the 8.15pm Kettering-Leicester on December 19, returning next morning on the 7.00am Melton Mowbray-Kettering. In December the prototype 'Deltic' was launched on a Liverpool-Euston main line roster covering the 10.10am up 'Merseyside Express' and the 4.55pm down 'Shamrock'. In the North-East the first Westinghouse pump-fitted Class 9 2-10-0s were drafted to Tyne Dock for the Consett ore trains at the end of the year. Among withdrawals in the final months of the year one noted particularly the extinction of the last ex-LNWR Webb 2-4-2Ts.

The year ended on an anxious note with announcement of BR's first large-scale main-line diesel orders, gloomy forecasts of increasing financial losses and — more immediately disturbing — with an appalling sequence of accidents, culminating in three affecting passenger trains within two days. Such was public unease that the newly-appointed Minister of Transport, Harold (now Lord) Watkinson, who had just succeeded John (now Lord) Boyd-Carpenter in the Tory administration, summoned the full BTC to special Saturday conclave with senior Ministry officials. Ironically, the Ministry had only just published its annual safety report proclaiming that not a passenger had been killed in a train accident during 1954.

The chronicle of disaster opened on the WR on Sunday, November 20, when 'Britannia' Pacific No 70026 on a Treherbert-Paddington excursion plunged down an embankment at Milton, near Didcot, with the first three coaches of its train; 11 were killed and many seriously hurt. The Pacific had been switched to the goods loop for engineering works. Proper warning had been given in the weekly notice, but the driver had overlooked the item; he had also missed the signals and consequently hit the turnout at around 50mph. He claimed he had not heard any siren from his Western ATC gear, but the Inspecting Officer was confident that it did function and that either driver or fireman unthinkingly re-set the apparatus and ignored its advice.

Within a fortnight 13 more died in a horrible affair on the SR at Barnes on December 2 (incidentally, two London Transport District Line trains had collided in fog at Bromley-by-Bow only the previous evening). Irregular manipulation of the Sykes lock-and-block apparatus by the Barnes signalman, forgetful of a train in section on his down local line, allowed a late-evening Waterloo-Windsor emu to run into the rear of a steam-hauled Battersea-Brent goods. Electric arcing quickly set the wooden body of the 1935-built emu's first coach ablaze, and this caused most of the fatalities.

The next two accidents occurred on the same day, December 22. In the early hours another infringement of signalling rules at Hellifield led to a 'Royal Scot' on the 9.15pm St Pancras-Glasgow sleeper running at about 25mph into the rear of the 9.15pm St Pancras-Edinburgh, fortunately without serious casualties as two bogie brakes at the rear of the latter train absorbed most of the impact. Then, in the early evening, the driver of a Class 5 4-6-0 on the 7.10pm St Pancras-Derby missed the Luton distant, caught the adverse home signal far too late to obey it properly, and ran into the 6.45pm St Pancras-Leicester in the station, killing one passenger. The very next evening the driver of SR Class N15X 4-6-0 No 32327 on the 7.45pm Waterloo-Basingstoke misread the Maybury intermediate signals between West Byfleet and Woking and collided at low speed with a Portsmouth line emu stopped at signals outside Woking station, fortunately without serious casualty. All in all, it was a far from merry Christmas for railwaymen in 1955.

The 'Devon Belle' with beaver-tail Pullman Observation Car at the rear.
Photo: P. M. Alexander.

Above: BR's experimental small diesel-electric branch line prototype No 10800 at Birmingham, New Street on 21 February 1955. Shedded at the time at Rugby, this 827hp engine worked to Birmingham and Peterborough.
Photo: C. F. H. Oldham.

Below: *Duke of Gloucester* leaving Crewe with a northbound express.
Photo: J. Ellson.

Upper left: Lickey incline unbanked train test, 6 March 1955. Load 220 tons, locomotive Class 5 MT 4-6-0 No 44776. First run (start from Stoke Works passing Bromsgrove station at 30 mph). Train seen here nearing Blackwell.

Middle left: Second run (stop and restart on incline at milepost 55). Train re-starting as laid down.

Lower left: Third run (start from Bromsgrove station).

Above: Lickey incline unbanked train test, 13 March 1955. Load 252 tons, locomotive 'Jubilee' class 4-6-0 No 45554 *Ontario*. First run (start from Stoke Works passing Bromsgrove station at 30 mph). Train seen here nearing Blackwell.

Below: Third run (stop and re-start on incline at mile post 55). The locomotive failed to re-start on first stop and backed train to Bromsgrove station for another try. It is seen here passing milepost 55 after this second attempt.

Photos: W. A. Camwell.

Left: A Western Region train behind 2-6-0
No 5378 and an unknown 28XX 2-8-0 at
Llanvihangel.
Photo: P. M. Alexander.

Right: A push-and-pull train in the West Midlands.
Ex LNWR Webb 5ft 6in 2-4-2 tank No 46654 at
Dudley Port station with a train for Dudley. March
1955.
Photo: P. B. Whitehouse.

Below: Webb 2-4-2T No 46654 leaving Dudley
Port junction with the 'Dudley Dodger' in March
1955.
Photo: P. B. Whitehouse.

Right: LMS 'Flying Pig' 2-6-0 No 43009 passing Curthwaite on the one-time Maryport & Carlisle Railway with a Workington to Carlisle race special on 9 April 1955.
Photo: W. A. Camwell.

Below: The Southern 1750 h.p. 1Co-Co1 twins of 1951 with the down 'Royal Scot' passing Greskine box, April 1955.
Photo: W. J. V. Anderson.

Lower right: Many of the Waterloo to Bournemouth services were in the hands of the light Bulleid Pacifics of 1955. Here is No 34041 Wilton at Bournemouth West on 11 April of that year.
Photo: C. F. H. Oldham.

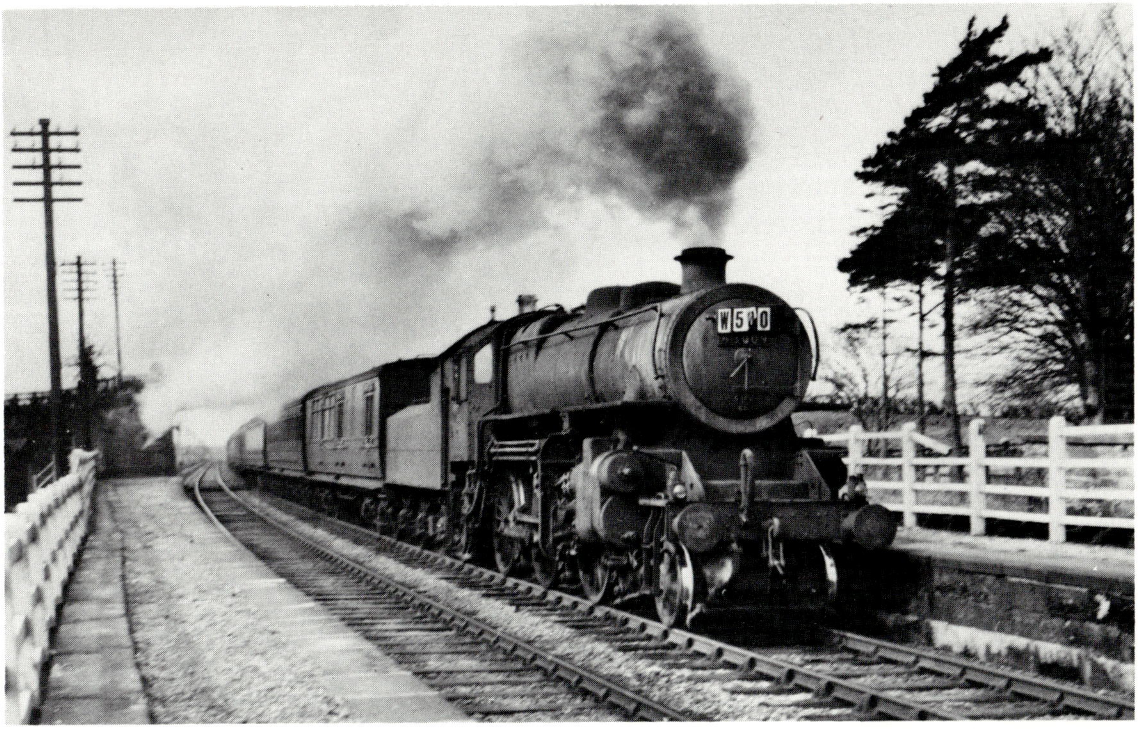

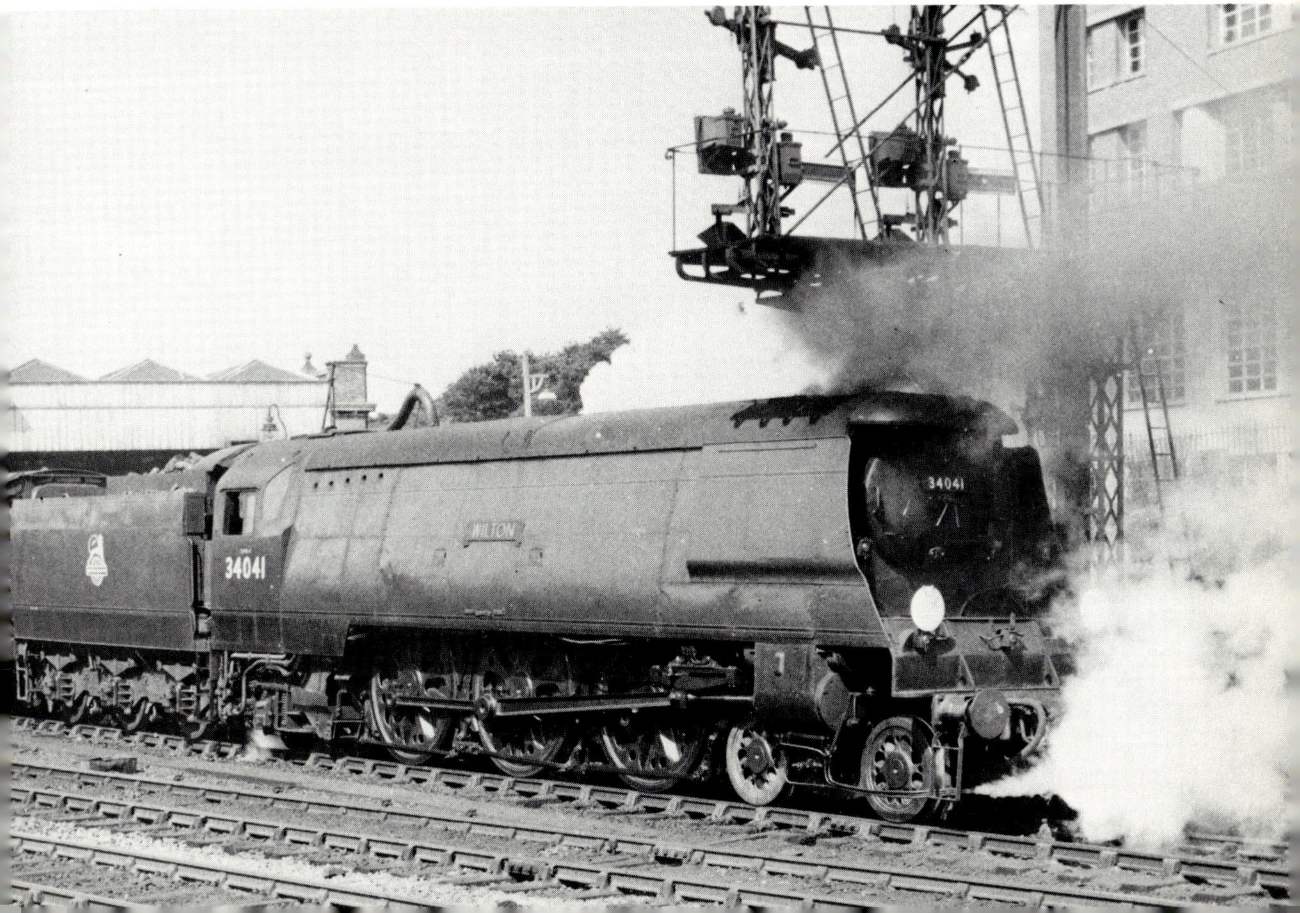
34041
WILTON
34041

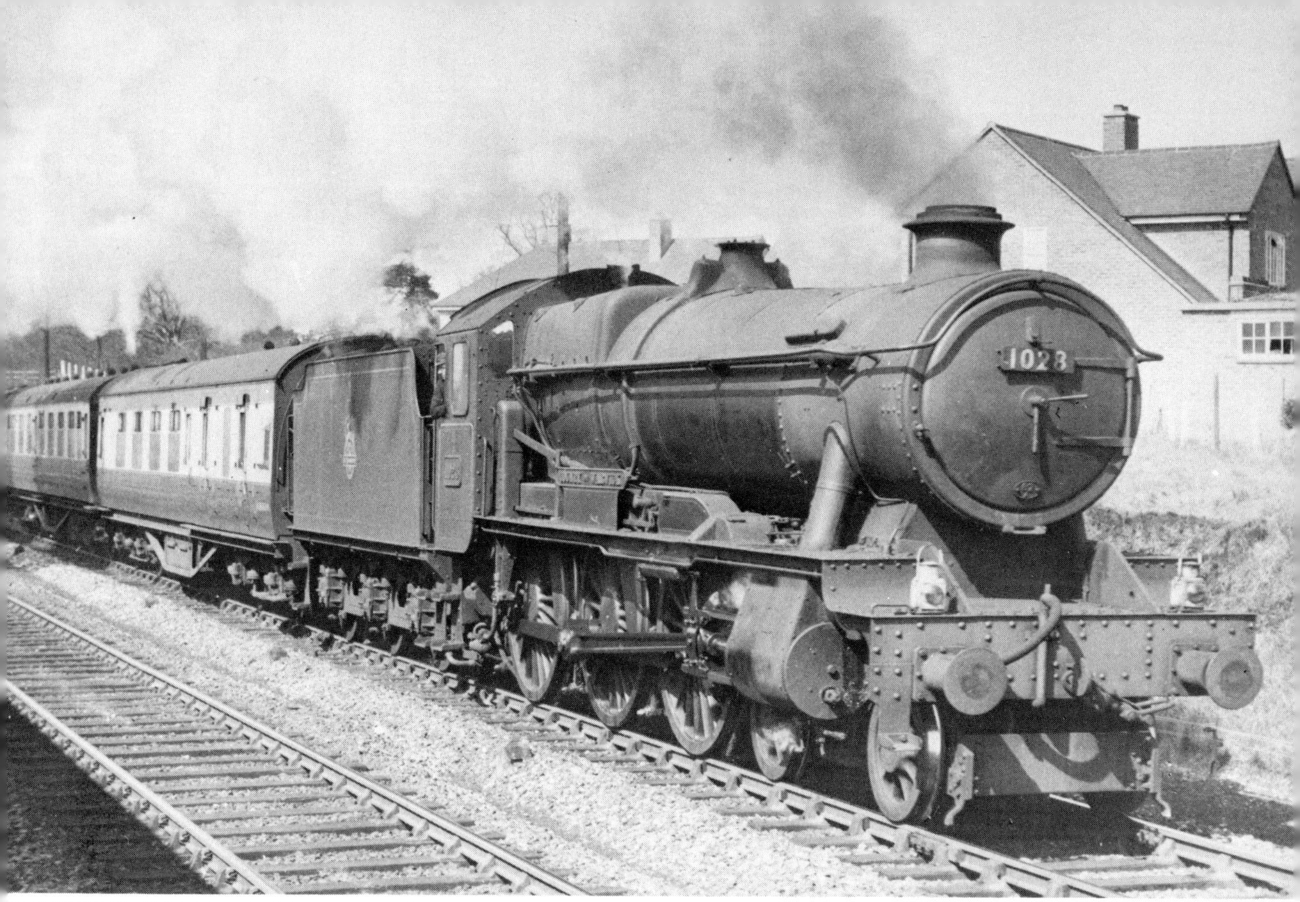
1023

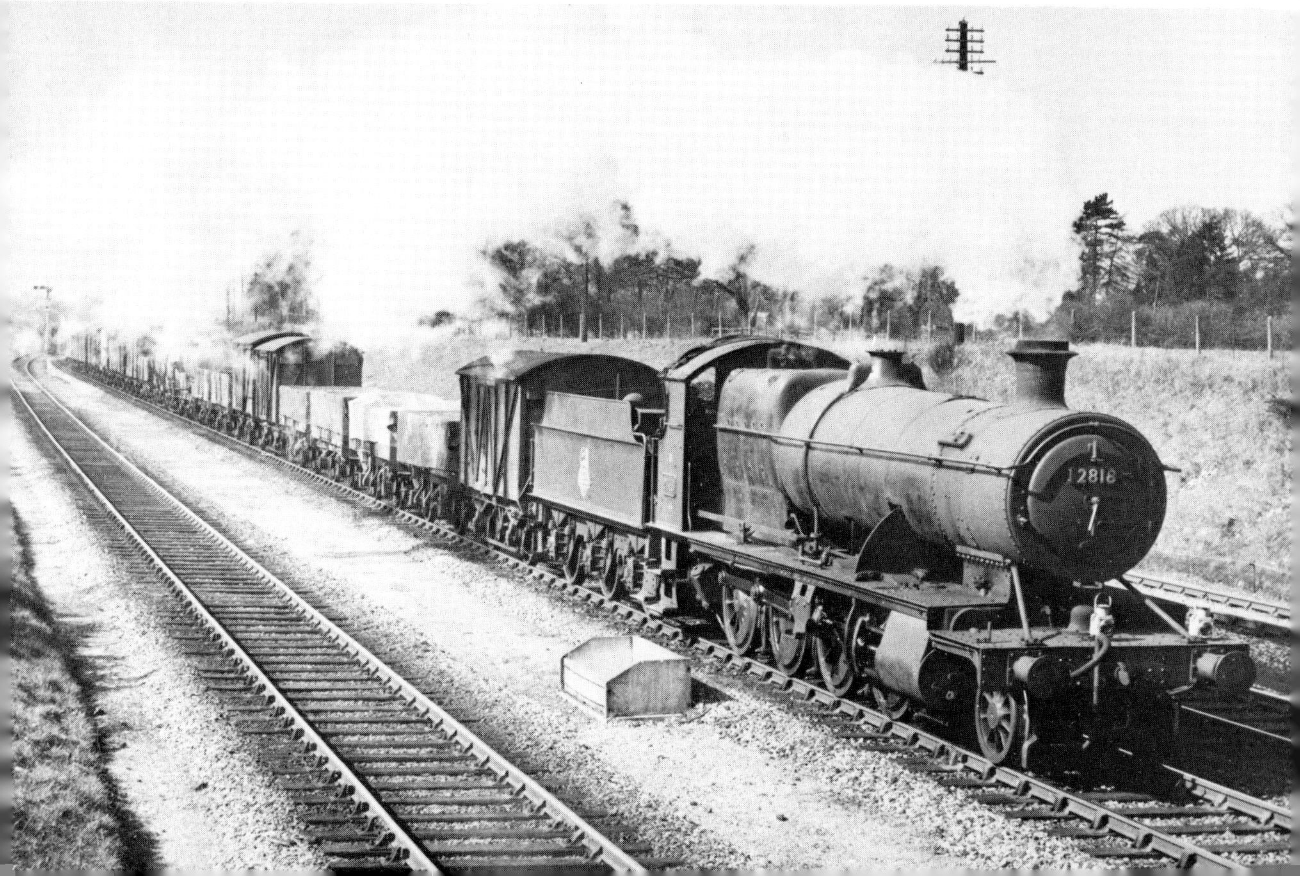
2818

Upper left: Hawksworth's GWR 'County' class 4-6-0 No 1028 *County of Warwick* with an up express passing Bentley Heath near Knowle & Dorridge on 16 April 1955.
Photo: C. F. H. Oldham.

Above: Fowler 2-6-4T No 42381 at Poynton with the Manchester (London Road) to Macclesfield and Uttoxeter train on 30 April 1955.
Photo: W. A. Camwell.

Lower left: GWR Churchward 2-8-0 No 2818 with a Bordesley Junction to Oxford freight train near Bentley Heath on 16 April 1955.
Photo: C. F. H. Oldham.

Below: LMS 'Mickey Mouse' 2-6-2T No 41282 with the 4.44 pm push-and-pull train from Delph to Oldham (Clegg Street) at Grotton and Springfield station on 30 April 1955 — the last day of service.
Photo: W. A. Camwell.

Thompson B1 class 4-6-0 No 61020 *Gemsbok* with a down express near Ripley in April 1955.
Photo: C. F. H. Oldham.

The 1955-introduced push-and-pull train service from Birmingham, New Street to Sutton Coldfield and Four Oaks gave an hourly off-peak train and was a preparation for the dmus to come. Later, LMS standard 'Mickey Mouse' 2-6-2T No 1224 of Monument Lane shed enters New Street with the 2.48 p.m. from Sutton on 7 May 1955.
Photo: C. F. H. Oldham.

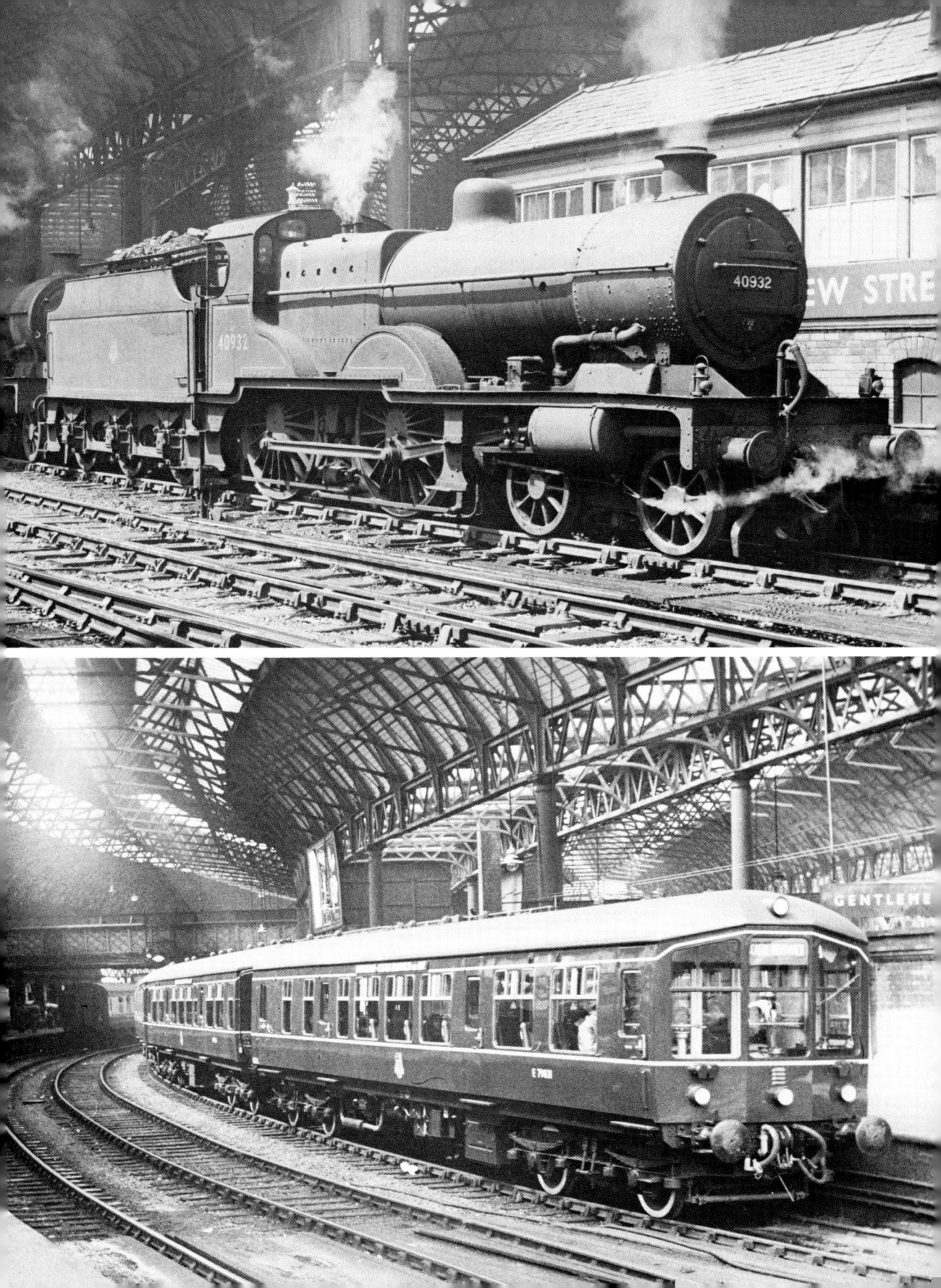

Upper left: The LMS Compound 4-4-0s were still busy on main line work in the Birmingham area. No 40932 pilots one of her unknown sisters on a Bristol–bound express on 19 May 1955. Photo: C. F. H. Oldham.

Lower left: Brand new Derby-built dmu with indicator "Castle Bromwich", for service to the then "British Industries Fair" at New Street Station, Birmingham on 11 May 1955. Photo: C. F. H. Oldham.

Above: Nationalisation brought one or two odd workings to delight the enthusiast. One of these was the London Brick Company's special headed by an ex-LNWR Super D 0-8-0 on Hatton bank during May 1955. Photo: P. B. Whitehouse.

Below: Class B16/3 4-6-0 No 61420 pounding northwards through Rugby with an evening freight on 18 May 1955.

Below: Still very much in the land of the living, ex-LMS 2-6-0+0-6-2 Garratt with a freight train, away from her normal haunts, passing York. Summer, 1955.
Photo: Eric Treacy.

Right: Normal working on the Lickey incline — two standard LMS 0-6-0 tanks — soon to be replaced by GWR-design 84XX pannier tanks.
Photo: P. B. Whitehouse.

Above: The up 'Thames-Clyde Express' leaving
Carlisle double-headed by Class 5 MT 4-6-0
No 45481 and an unknown 'Jubilee'.
Photo: Eric Treacy.

Overleaf: The down 'Thames-Clyde Express'
passing Leeds Wortley Junction behind rebuilt
Royal Scot class 4-6-0 No 46113 Cameronian.
Photo: Eric Treacy.

Upper right: Class A4 4-6-2 No 60023 Golden
Eagle heads the down 'Flying Scotsman'.
Photo: P. M. Alexander

Lower Right: The 'Tees-Tyne Pullman' hauled by A4
Pacific No 60003 Andrew K. McCosh crosses King
Edward Bridge, Newcastle.
Photo: Eric Treacy.

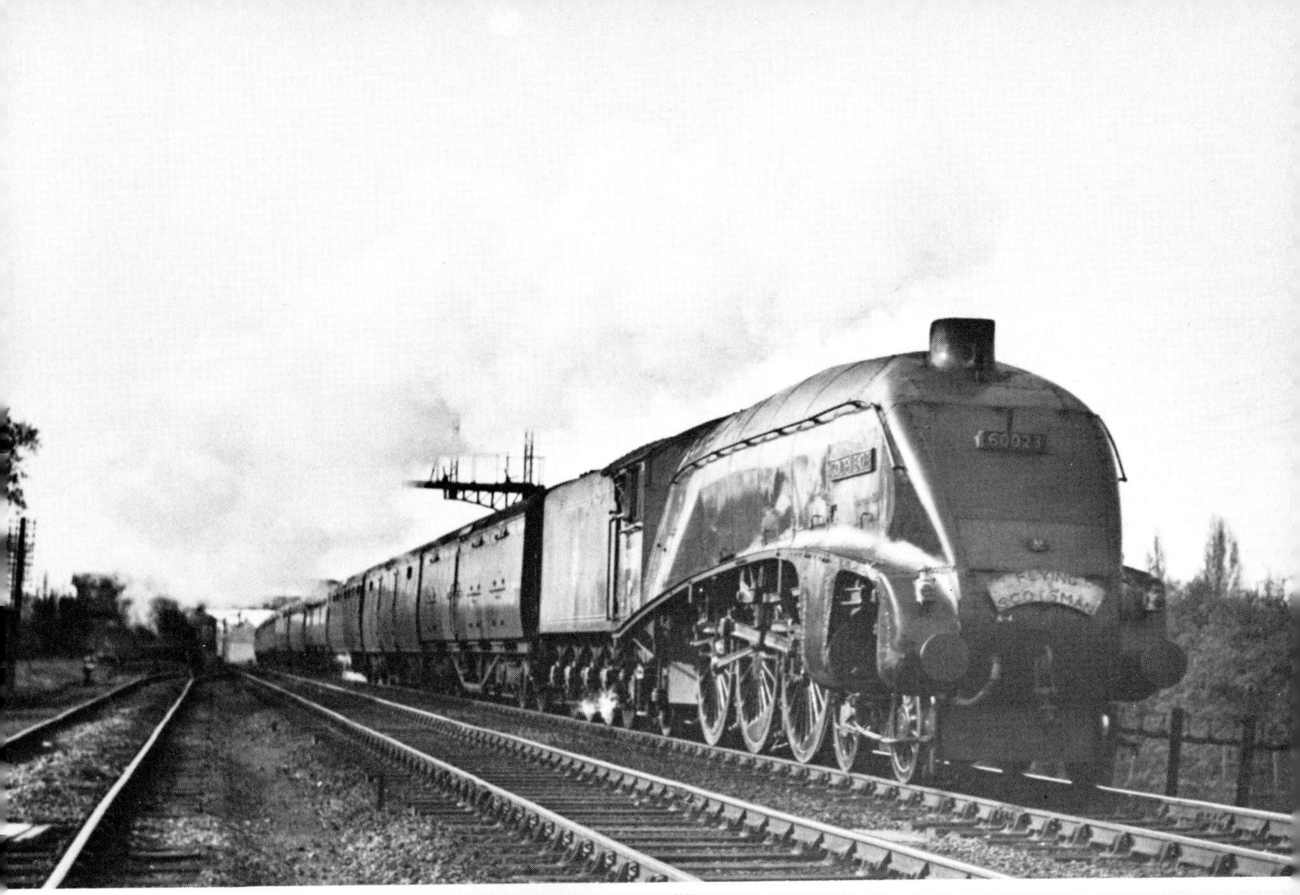
60023
FLYING SCOTSMAN

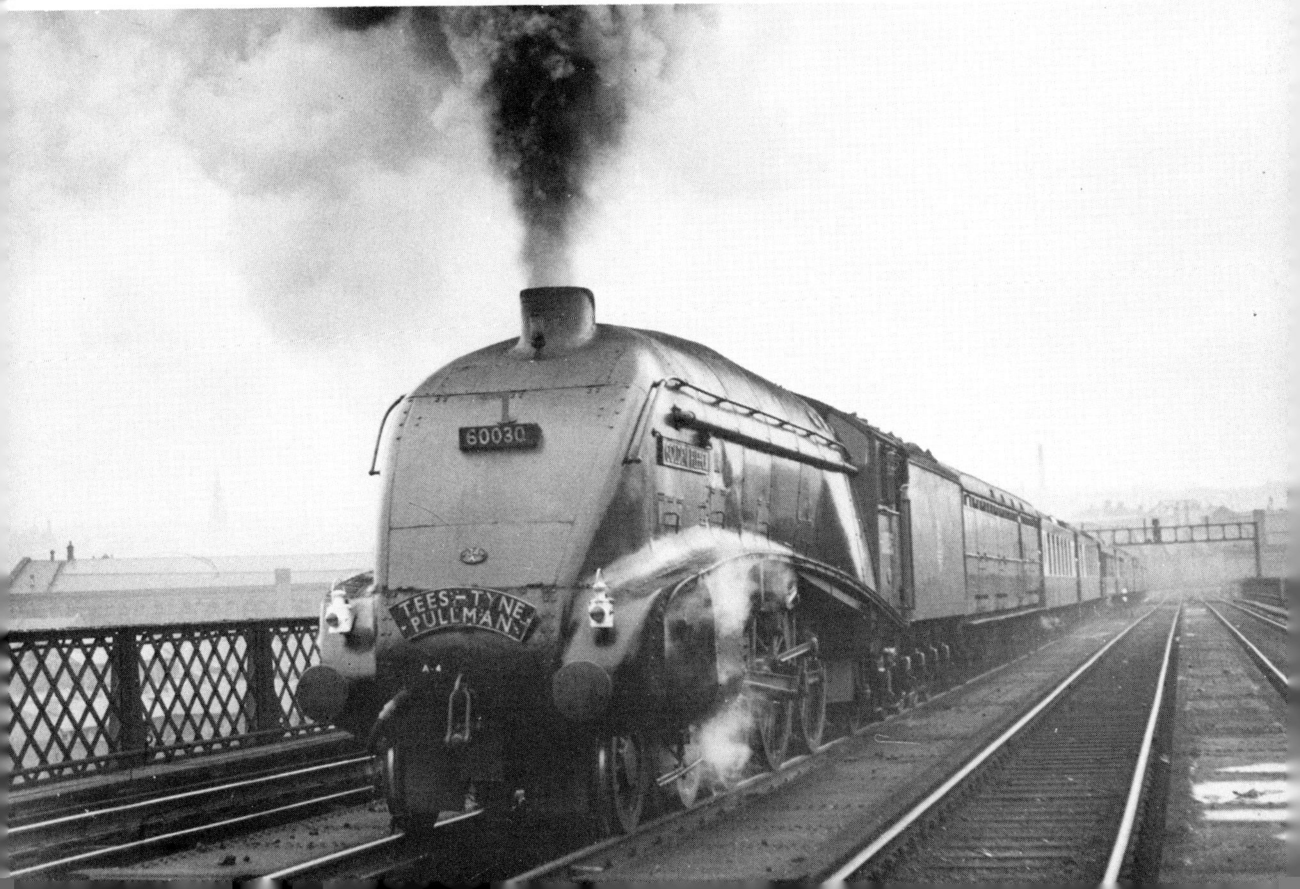
60030
TEES-TYNE PULLMAN

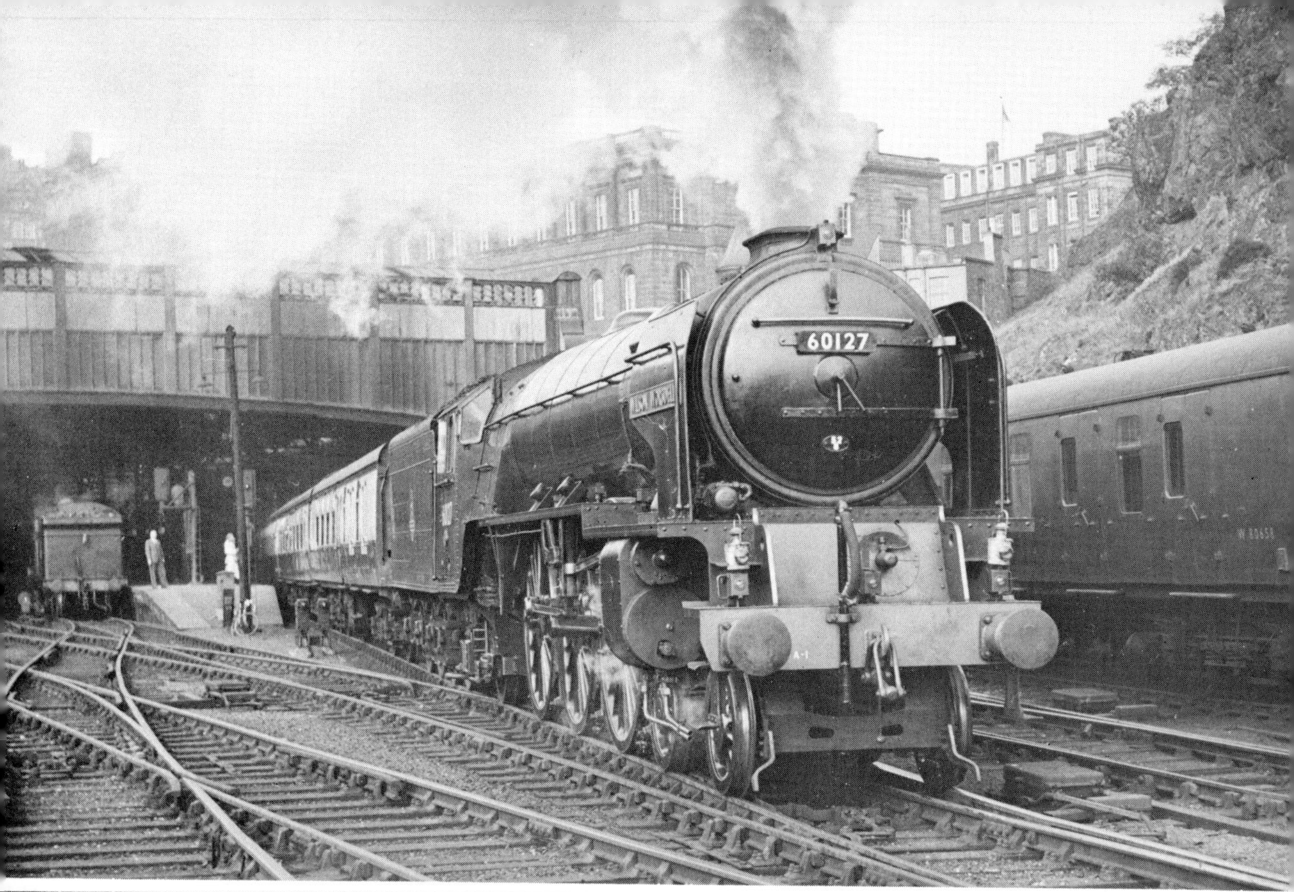
60127

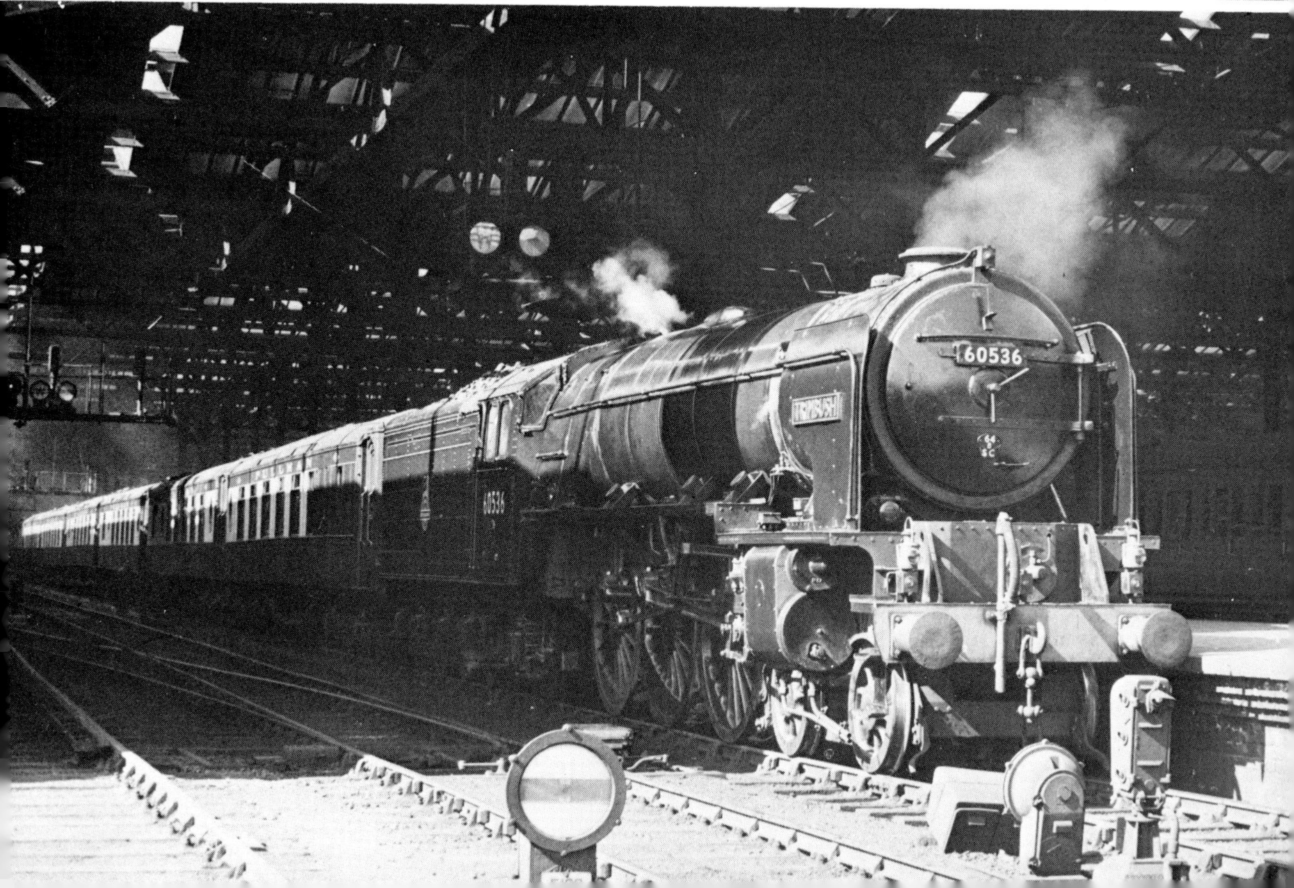
60536

Upper left: The up 'Flying Scotsman' leaving
Edinburgh Waverley station behind A1 Pacific
No 60127 *Wilson Worsdell.*
Photo: Eric Treacy.

Lower left: The down 'Queen of Scots' Pullman at
Edinburgh Waverley station behind A2 Pacific
No 60536 *Trimbush.*
Photo: Eric Treacy.

Above: Down 'Golden Arrow' at Victoria station,
London. The engine is the locomotive specially
furbished for the Festival of Britain Exhibition,
'Britannia' Pacific No 70004 *William Shakespeare.*
Photo: Eric Treacy.

Upper left: Newton Abbot to Exeter train
approaching Starcross on 6 June 1955.
Locomotive is No 5548.
Photo: P. B. Whitehouse.

Middle left: Exeter to Kingswear train between
Goodrington and Churston on 17 June 1955. GWR
small-wheeled 45XX 2-6-2T.
Photo: P. B. Whitehouse.

Lower left: 'Castle class' 4-6-0 No 4091 *Dudley
Castle* on the sea wall near Shaldon, Devon, with
an up express on 6 June 1955.
Photo: P. B. Whitehouse.

Above: The new BR Standard Class 2 2-6-0s soon
penetrated into the hills of Wales. Here is
No 78007 on the Cambrian Coast line at
Penychain on 23 June 1955.
Photo: C. F. H. Oldham.

Below: At long last the GWR 4-4-0s, 0-6-0s and
2-6-2 tanks began to be ousted from the Cambrian
Coast line. Here is BR Class 2 2-6-0 No 78033
near Criccieth on 21 June 1955.
Photo: C. F. H. Oldham.

Above: The Abermule to Kerry branch was rarely used during the 1950s but one of the remaining (in fact the last in service) Dean Goods 0-6-0s was kept for occasional working up the line. Here is No 2538 at Kerry in June 1955.
Photo: P. B. Whitehouse.

Upper right: Eastleigh shed, June 1955. Class B4 0-4-0T No 30096.
Photo: P. B. Whitehouse.

Middle right: Eastleigh shed, June 1955. Class T9 4-4-0 No 30117.
Photo: P. B. Whitehouse.

Below: 'Dukedog' class 4-4-0 No 9003 at Pwllheli on 26 June 1955.
Photo: C. F. H. Oldham.

Lower right: One of the L Class 4-4-0 'Germans' No 31781 leaves Margate with a London to Ramsgate train.
Photo: P. B. Whitehouse.

Above: The Riddles-designed 'Austerity' 2-8-0s were still hard at work on the main lines during 1955. Here is No 90100 near Ripley on 30 June 1955.
Photo: C. F. H. Oldham.

Upper right: New steam power coming off the production lines included 10 Crosti-boilered 9F class 2-10-0s. Here is No 92020 outside Crewe paint shop.
Photo: J. Ellson.

Lower right: Another Crosti-boilered class 9F 2-10-0 at Saltley shed.
Photo: J. Ellson.

Upper left: Both fitted with standard LNWR-type chimneys, these ex-North London Railway 0-6-0Ts await a Stephenson Locomotive Society special at Middleton Top.
Photo: P. B. Whitehouse.

Above: Workmen's train approaching Old Hill (Worcs) behind GWR 0-6-0PT No 7435 — number still on the bufferbeam.
Colourviews Picture Library.

Middle left: Halesowen station, Worcestershire, in June 1955. GWR 74XX 0-6-0PT with train for Longbridge. This branch was still in use throughout its length for two daily workmen's passenger trains from Longbridge (for the Austin Works) to Old Hill.
Photo: P. B. Whitehouse.

Below: Birmingham-Bournemouth train climbing towards Masbury Summit on the old Somerset & Dorset Joint line, behind Class 2 4-4-0 No 40569 and new standard Class 3 No 76012.
Photo: P. B. Whitehouse.

Lower left: Hayling Island terminus, July 1955, with ex-LBSCR Terrier 0-6-0T No 32677.
Photo: P. B. Whitehouse

45

Above: Ex-NER 4-6-2T No 69853 with the 10.05 a.m. train from South Shields to Sunderland at East Boldon on 12 July 1955.
Photo: W. A. Camwell.

Upper right: A northbound goods climbing Beattock Bank behind 'Jubilee' class 4-6-0 No 45715 *Invincible*.
Photo: W. J. V. Anderson.

Lower right: The last LMS Royal Scot to be fitted with a taper boiler No 46137 *The Prince of Wales's Volunteers South Lancashire*, was converted at Crewe in 1955.
Photo: J. R. Paterson.

Below: Glasgow (Queen Street) to St Andrews and Dundee train at Largo (Fife Coast Line) behind B1 class 4-6-0 No 61103 on 13 July 1955.
Photo: W. A. Camwell.

Above & Below: The two LMS prototype diesel-electric locomotives, Nos 10000/1, in Derby Works yard. In 1955 BR had only seven main-line DE units.
Photo: J. Ellson.

Above: BR No 71000 *Duke of Gloucester* on trial
with the Swindon dynamometer car.
Photo: Ian Allan Library.

Below: Unrebuilt West Country No 34016 *Bodmin*
with the 'Atlantic Coast Express'.
Photo: P. M. Alexander.

Above: An un-named BR 'Britannia' Pacific with a down express on the old LNWR main line near Cathion, Warwickshire, on 23 July 1955.
Photo: C. F. H. Oldham.

Left: Midland Class 2P 4-4-0 No 40556 with the 10.50 a.m. Manchester Central to Chinley train at Romiley (Mid & GC Joint) on 14 July 1955.
Photo: W. A. Camwell.

Below: Tewksbury Branch train at Upton-on-Severn station behind a Midland Railway 0-4-4 tank No 58071.
Photo: P. B. Whitehouse.

Above: Crab 2-6-0 No 42935 at New Mills with the 7.27 a.m. Manchester (London Road) to Buxton all stations train on 19 July 1955. Photo: W. A. Camwell.

Below: GWR 0-6-0PT No 6436 with the afternoon train from Abergavenny Junction to Merthyr at Clydach Halt on 22 July 1955. A Great Western intrusion into ex-LNWR territory. Photo: W. A. Camwell.

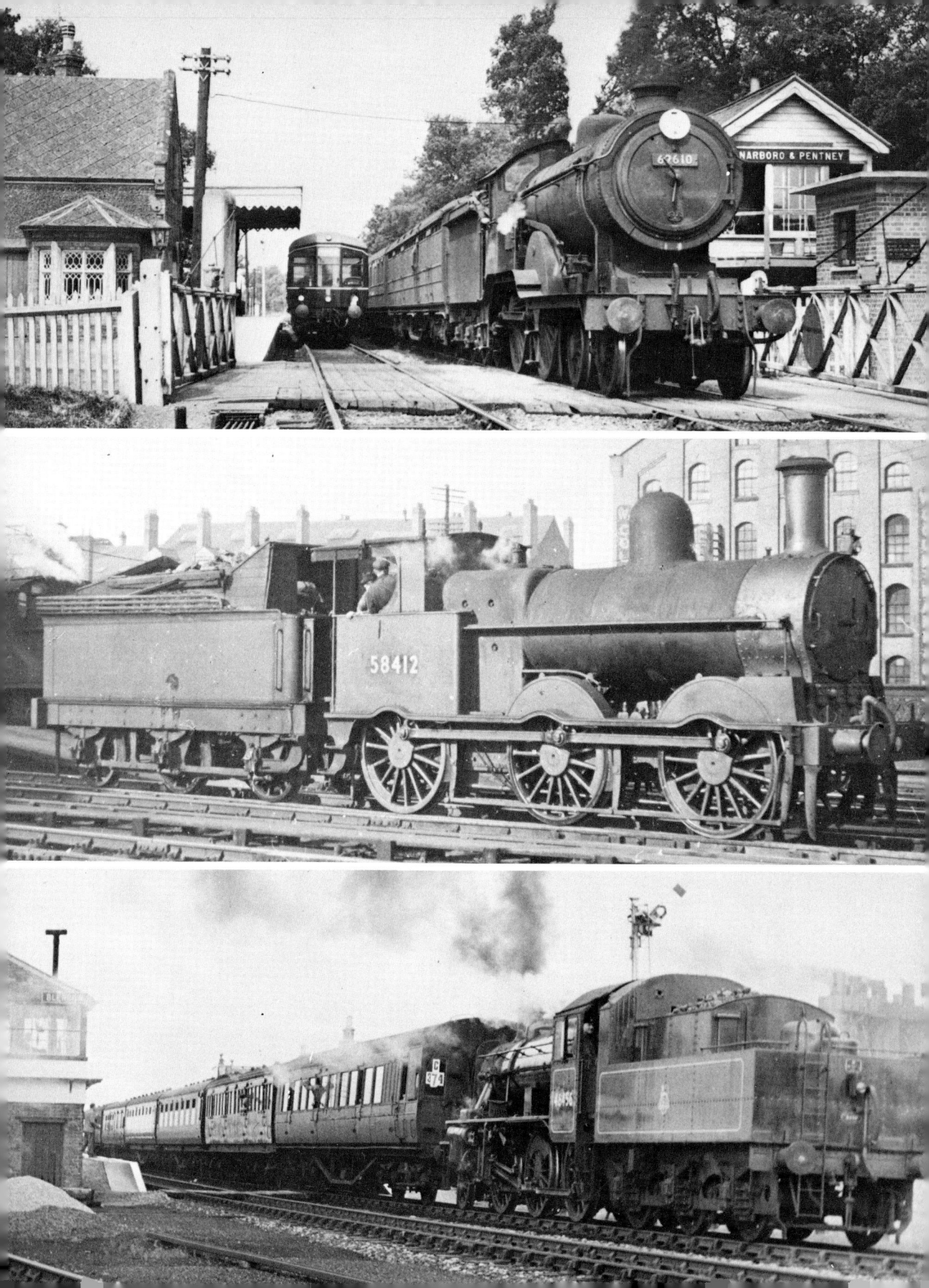

Above: Two N Class 2-6-0s at Reading (SR) shed. August 1955.
Photo: P. B. Whitehouse.

Upper left: LNER (ex-GE) 4-4-0 No 62610 at Narborough and Pentney with the 12.42 p.m. train from Kings Lynn to Dereham on 2 August 1955. The line became dieselised from 19 September 1955 and dmus E79038 and 79254 are shown here, on the left-hand side, on trial.
Photo: W. A. Camwell.

Middle left: One of the very last of the Webb 18in goods or 'Cauliflower' 0-6-0s to remain in service — No 58412, ousted from the Workington-Penrith-Carlisle lines in 1955.
Photo: D. J. Sutton.

Lower left: Brand-new out of works, this LMS-designed Class 2 2-6-0 No 46456 takes the 11 a.m. Penrith-Workington train out of Blencow on 5 August 1950. O. S. Nock is on the footplate. This class finally ousted the LNWR Cauliflowers.
Photo: P. B. Whitehouse.

Right: Ex SE&CR Class D 4-4-0 No 31488 at Reading in August 1955.
Photo: P. B. Whitehouse.

GWR Churchward 2-6-0 No 7305 near Mickleton (Campden bank) with an Oxford freight on 8 August 1955.

Photo: C. F. H. Oldham.

The 'Cornish Riviera Express' operated in 1955 with a four-hour Paddington to Plymouth timing. No 6008 *King James II* takes the down train west of Brent. Photo: D. S. Fish.

Above: Class K1 2-6-0 No 62012 piloting ex-NBR 4-4-0 No 62482 *Glen Mamie* with train running along the foothills of Ben Nevis en route to Craigendoran and Glasgow.
Photo: P. B. Whitehouse.

Upper right: Ex Caledonian Railway Pickersgill 4-4-0 No 54494 working as banker between Blair Athol and Dalnaspidal summit in August 1955.
Photo: P. B. Whitehouse.

Middle right: Dalnaspidal Station. The same engine coupled on to the train as pilot after the failure of the Stanier Class 5 4-6-0.
Photo: P. B. Whitehouse.

Lower right: For a short while the Caledonian Class 3 0-6-0s were used on passenger trains over the Speyside branch of the old GN of S whilst the larger-wheeled indigenous 4-4-0s were relegated to freight work.
Photo: P. B. Whitehouse.

Below: Fort William Shed, August 1955.
Photo: P. B. Whitehouse.

Upper left: On busy summer Saturdays in 1955 the Lymington Pier to Waterloo trains were still in charge of LSWR T9 4-4-0s. Here is No 30117 approaching the main line in August 1955.
Photo: P. B. Whitehouse.

Middle left: Churchward 2-6-0s were once the mainstay of the Ruabon-Barmouth branch but were ousted with the coming of the Manors. Occasionally one was still at work in its old haunts, as No 4377, seen here with a Saturday relief express passing Berwyn in August 1955.
Photo: P. B. Whitehouse.

Lower left: During 1955 old standard types in the form of GWR 2-6-2 tanks were still to be found regularly at work on the Cambrian Coast line.
Photo: P. B. Whitehouse.

Above: The same month No 4377 is seen here with the up 'Cambrian Coast Express' near Caersws.
Photo: P. B. Whitehouse.

Below: GWR 0-4-2T No 1432 with the 3.25 p.m. train from Wrexham to Ellesmere at Bangor-on-Dee on 1 October 1955.
Photo: W. A. Camwell.

BR Standard class 2-6-2 tank No 82005 on the Western Region near Dawlish on 11 September 1955.
Photo: C. F. H. Oldham.

Ex-GWR 'Hall' class No 6956 climbing Hatton bank near Warwick with a down Oxford express on 9 July 1955. The "Syphon G" van is still in GWR brown but the coaches carry the BR red and cream colours reminiscent of the County Donegal Railways Joint Committee.
Photo: C. F. H. Oldham.

Above: Early days of enthusiast-run tourist railways. The newly acquired 0-4-0 WT *Douglas* at Dolgoch station, Talyllyn Railway on 21 September, 1955.
Colourviews Picture Library.

Upper right: This somewhat sombre picture shows BR's Vale of Rheidol line as it really was in the early and middle 1950s — dull and unenterprising. It was not until 1957/58 that the engines were repainted and named and the stock decked out in chocolate and cream once more. In 1955 the locomotives were just dirty and the stock, under the grime, red and cream.
Photo: P. B. Whitehouse.

Lower right: Early days of enthusiast-run tourist railways. The historic locomotive *Prince* with train at the Harbour Station Portmadoc on 19 September 1955.
Colourviews Picture Lirary.

A typical branch line scene of the mid-1950s. Ex-LSWR M7 0-4-4T No 30047 on the 3.46 pm from Midhurst to Petersfield, photographed near Petersfield.
Photo: P .M. Alexander.